PSALMS

An Honor-Shame Paraphrase
of 15 Psalms

JAYSON GEORGES

Series Endorsements

"The Honor-Shame Paraphrase series gives us a fresh look at an ancient perspective. As a paraphrase, each book nicely serves as a middle ground between a commentary and a translation. Accordingly, they aptly highlight diverse and subtle ways that honor and shame influence the biblical writers. One easily sees the care given to remain biblically faithful and culturally meaningful. I commend this series both as a useful tool for personal study and public ministry."

—**Dr. Jackson Wu**, professor to Chinese pastors, author of *Saving God's Face*

"Applying shame and honor as ever present realities in the ancient world, Jayson Georges powerfully accents the cultural values behind the words that would otherwise seem flavorless. His paraphrasing penetrates deeply into the intentions of the heart that often lay hidden from readers. We are exposed to life as it was lived, feelings as they were felt and hidden motives as they were brought to light. The biblical text breathes afresh with meaning."

—**Dr. Duane H. Elmer**, Emeritus Distinguished Professor, Trinity Evangelical Divinity School, author of *Cross-Cultural Servanthood*

"In a rapidly globalizing world cultural differences are confronting us daily. Not only have these cultural differences exposed a cultural bias in our daily lives, but they have also exposed the significant role culture plays in our approach to the Bible. The Honor-Shame Paraphrase provides a great resource that helps people understand how the Bible would have been understood in the Ancient Near East. I am both thankful and excited to recommend a resource that will help us understand the Bible."

—**Spencer MacCuish**, President, Eternity Bible College

"This lively and engaging paraphrase of Esther, like all the biblical paraphrases in this series, seeks to illuminate and express key implicit cultural assumptions shaping biblical discourse. Sumptuous food and fabulous feasting, role violations and status reversals, male honoring and female defiance, enemy plotting and counter-cultural female heroics are all displayed here as strands of a fascinating story of honor denied and honor bestowed."

—**Dr. John H. Elliott**, Professor Emeritus, University of San Francisco, author of *1 Peter, Anchor Bible Commentary*

Psalms: An Honor-Shame Paraphrase of 15 Psalms

Timē Press

Table of Contents

Series Introduction

Anyone who reads the Bible today faces an unavoidable fact—Scripture was originally written in and for a culture different than our own culture. This makes understanding the Bible a challenge.

Consider the meaning of these words: *He whistled at her, and she winked back.* This sentence probably brought to mind an image of two people flirting. Your mind intuitively used cultural assumptions to interpret the facial gestures as innuendos. But depending on your cultural context, winking could mean something entirely different: in Asia, it is an offensive gesture; in West Africa, parents wink at children as a signal for them to leave the room. Interpretation is based on cultural assumptions, so we must recognize that the cultural gap between the biblical world and us may cause different interpretations.

You've heard this statistic: 90 percent of communication is non-verbal. This suggests that most meaning is *implicit*. Every writer assumes the reader can "read between the lines," so there is no need to state the obvious. As the example about winking illustrates, the sender and receiver of a message must share common cultural assumptions for communication to be effective. But when people from two *different* cultures try to communicate, meaning gets lost in translation. This explains why readers today might misinterpret aspects of the Bible—we don't share a common culture.

Biblical writers assumed their readers understood the implicit social values of honor-shame cultures, such as: patronage, hospitality, purity, ethnicity, family, reciprocity, etc. But modern readers don't intuitively know the assumed cultural nuances of ancient societies. So we misunderstand (or simply miss) aspects of the Bible because of cultural blindness. This problem is acute for Westerners because their guilt-innocence culture differs significantly from biblical cultures. Modern Western values such as legality, individualism, egalitarianism, and rationalism influence how we read the Bible, but they were not prominent in ancient cultures. (Christians in the Majority World do live in honor-shame cultures that are similar to biblical cultures. But, unfortunately, the traditions of Western Christianity unduly influence their theology.)

Cultural assumptions even affect the meaning of individual words. For example, the English word "faith" refers to someone's personal belief about something. This meaning reflects the rationalistic and individualistic values of Western culture. However, the biblical notion of "faith" reflects relational and collectivistic cultural values. In the Old Testament, an Israelite's "faith" is a commitment to their covenant obligation to honor Yahweh. Likewise, the New Testament word translated "faith" (Greek: *pistis*) suggests loyalty and fidelity to a relationship. Biblical faith is not merely "belief *about* God," but "allegiance *to* God." Western cultural values give the word "faith" a cognitive, individualistic meaning that distracts readers from the relational connotations of the biblical concept.

Reading the Bible across cultures can be difficult; however, the task is certainly not impossible. With cultural awareness, people today can accurately interpret the Bible by bridging the cultural gap between our world and the biblical world.

The Honor-Shame Paraphrase highlights the honor-shame dynamics of the Bible for modern readers by making explicit the implicit cultural assumptions of the Bible. This helps readers overcome cultural blindness and read between the lines. We show how original audiences heard the message in light of their shared cultural assumptions.

The Honor-Shame Paraphrase uses several strategies to express the cultural values and implications of the Bible. For example, we avoid clichéd religious words such as *holy*, *Christ*, and *faith*. These words are like dull knives: over usage has blunted their effect. So instead we use terms like *entirely acceptable* (holy), *God's exalted king* (Christ), and *complete loyalty* (faith). These re-definitions rescue truth from familiarity and accentuate the honor-shame nuances of the original words. The Honor-Shame Paraphrase also amplifies certain passages. This means inserting words or phrases in order to clarify the author's main point or logical connection. The goal throughout is to make the original, honor-shame meaning of the Bible more obvious for readers who do not share the same cultural assumptions. This is similar to how Ezra and the Levites "helped the people to understand the law . . . They read from the book, from the law of God, with interpretation. They gave the sense, so that the people understood the reading" (Neh 8:7b–8, NRSV).

Please do not equate this Honor-Shame Paraphrase with the actual Bible. This paraphrase is a *socio-cultural exposition* that seeks to illuminate (not translate) the Bible. The genre of paraphrase weaves together commentary and application to capture the message of the Bible in a fresh way (akin to Eugene Peterson's *The Message*). In this way, we make academic research about biblical cultures accessible and informative for people today.

Before the actual paraphrase, we first explain the socio-cultural context of the biblical book. This introduces the key cultural dynamics that are essential for understanding the book's rhetorical, social, and theological strategy. These cultural nuances shed light on the meaning and purpose of the biblical message.

Finally, honor-shame is not a "new lens" for reading the Bible but more like a shovel that removes centuries of residue. Honor and shame are inherent aspects of ancient cultures and biblical theology, not merely categories from modern anthropology. The Honor-Shame Paraphrase does not contextualize the Bible for a new setting. Rather it seeks to make the original meaning of the Bible more apparent for contemporary readers from a different culture. Nevertheless, we do hope this Honor-Shame Paraphrase offers you new biblical insights for life, ministry, and theology in today's world.

Introduction to Psalms

Honor and shame are profound emotions that people *feel*, not academic categories or cerebral ideas. People in all cultures use the figurative language of songs and poetry to express the deepest passions of their heart. For this reason, the book of Psalms—a collection of 150 ancient Hebrew songs and poems—offers a rich biblical perspective on honor and shame.

The Socio-Theological Context: Israel's Covenant

Readers should interpret the Psalms within the social context of covenant. Yahweh formed a special, reciprocal relationship with Israel at Mt. Sinai. He promised to protect and exalt Israel among all the other nations. In return, the people of Israel were expected to honor God with loyalty and obedience. This socio-cultural framework of covenant informs the theology of ancient Israel. The basic message of Psalms, in honor-shame terms, is that *the honorable God faithfully keeps his covenant by honoring his people and by shaming their enemies.* Most psalms either celebrate or lament this patron-client relationship between Yahweh and Israel.

When Israel experiences God's covenant faithfulness and favor (e.g., a strong king, military victory, economic prosperity, international renown), they rejoice and honor God. Salvation in the Psalms is not just forgiveness of sins and entrance into

13

heaven, but it also involves *vindication* of honor, *restoration* of status, *deliverance* from shame, and the *humiliation* of enemies. In response to this divine salvation, the psalmists honor God by recounting his faithful deeds. As God told Israel, "I will deliver you, and you shall glorify me" (50:15). Psalms of praise glorify God for his *benevolence, patronage, faithfulness, covenant loyalty, favor*, and *generosity* as a trustworthy covenant partner.

But when God's people experience shame, they call upon God to vindicate their status and humiliate their enemies. In moments of shame, Israelites feel betrayed by their covenant partner. God's apparent disloyalty jeopardizes the very relationship that defines Israel's identify and value. Psalms of lament plea with God to remember the covenant and rescue his people from disgrace.

Theological Motifs

Five theological motifs pervade the book of Psalms. The motifs center around God's covenant relationship with his people and flow out of an honor-shame worldview. To help us read Psalms from an honor-shame cultural perspective, the following sections examine these five theological motifs and provide examples from several Psalms. (All citations in this introduction are from the NRSV.)

14

1. The Honor of God

God is the ultimate source of honor. Humanity must look to God, not human strength, to be lifted up and honored. Yahweh alone blesses people with honor.

> But you, O Lord, are a shield around me,
>> my glory, and the one who lifts up my head. (3:3)

> On God rests my deliverance and my honor;
>> my mighty rock, my refuge is in God. (62:7a)

> For the Lord God is a sun and shield;
>> he bestows favor and honor. (84:11)

> I will rescue them and honor them. (91:15c)

In the Psalms, Israel's God is an honorable benefactor par excellence. Yahweh is a faithful and trustworthy patron. The Hebrew word *hesed* ("steadfast love") refers to God's covenant loyalty and constant patronage—virtues that define his character. God's concrete help for Israel demonstrates his trustworthiness and enhances his honor.

> I will sing of your steadfast love (*hesed*), O LORD, forever;
>> with my mouth I will proclaim your faithfulness to all
>> generations. (89:1)

> O give thanks to the LORD, for he is good,
>
> for his steadfast love (*hesed*) endures forever. (136:1)

Along with being faithful, God is powerful. In traditional cultures, a central aspect of leadership is establishing and maintaining the social order. Respected leaders can exalt or demote people as they please. The God of the Psalms has authority to determine the social hierarchy and put everything where it belongs. At creation, God vanquished mythical gods and imposed his social order in the world (74:12–17). During the exodus and conquest of Canaan, God demoted other nations and exalted his people Israel. The sovereignty of God means he can grant favor and honor to whom he desires.

> But it is God who executes judgment,
>
> putting down one and lifting up another. (75:6–7)

But that divine order deteriorated, thus leading to moments of defeat and exile. God's failure to honor Israelites made him appear weak, disloyal, and shameful. So psalmists ask God to exercise his sovereign authority and put everything back in place. In the proper social hierarchy, God sits enthroned above the heavens as the ultimate ruler, and his people Israel (co-)rule over creation.

> You have made [human beings] a little lower than God,
>
> and crowned them with glory and honor.

You have given them dominion over the works of your hands. (8:5–6)

Because God grants honor, remains loyal, and sovereignly establishes order, he is worthy of praise. God's clients—the recipients of his favor—repay him with honor. The people of Israel express their gratitude, declare their allegiance to his rule, and sing his praises. God's people magnify his supreme glory throughout the world. Many psalms are acts of praise that honor God for his faithful character and benevolent actions. In the reciprocal covenant relationship, God enhances his own reputation when he preserves an Israelite's honor, as that person will repay him with thanks and honor.

> Ascribe to the LORD the glory of his name;
>   worship the LORD in holy splendor. (29:1–2)

> I will give thanks to you, O Lord, among the peoples;
>   I will sing praises to you among the nations.
> For your steadfast love is as high as the heavens;
>   your faithfulness extends to the clouds.
> Be exalted, O God, above the heavens.
>   Let your glory be over all the earth. (57:9–11)

> O give thanks to the LORD, call on his name,
>   make known his deeds among the peoples.
> Sing to him, sing praises to him;

tell of all his wonderful works.

Glory in his holy name. (105:1–3)

As the supreme king, God's glory *must* be declared and exalted. All creation praises his name, plus God himself acts for the sake of his own glory. The honor challenges of blasphemous enemies demand that God vindicate his name and assert his status.

Is the enemy to revile your name forever? . . .
Remember this, O LORD, how the enemy scoffs,
    and an impious people reviles your name. (74:10a, 18)

[God] saved them for his name's sake,
    so that he might make known his mighty power. (106:8)

2. The Shamefulness of People

The book of Psalms portrays the default state of humanity as one of lowly shame. Compared to the eternality of God, humans are a shadow, a breath, withering grass, dirt. These metaphors symbolize the insignificance and innate shamefulness experienced by humans after the Fall.

Those of low estate are but a breath,
    those of high estate are a delusion;
in the balances they go up;
    they are together lighter than a breath. (62:9)

For he knows how we were made;

he remembers that we are dust.

As for mortals, their days are like grass. (103:14–15)

O Lᴏʀᴅ, what are human beings that you regard them,

or mortals that you think of them?

They are like a breath;

their days are like a passing shadow. (144:3–4)

Besides human mortality and weakness, another source of shame is sin—our failure to rightly honor God. The enemies of God boast in their perceived greatness and take pride in their earthly honor (10:3–4). This arrogance diminishes God's glory and brings people to a state of shame.

All the peoples behold his glory.

All worshipers of images are put to shame,

those who make their boast in worthless idols;

all gods bow down before him. (96:6–7)

Even as God's chosen people, Israel defamed God's name. Psalms 78, 105, and 106 are confessions of Israel's unfaithfulness. The nation has been a disloyal client toward Yahweh. Despite God's faithfulness, Israel has disobeyed his word, been unthankful, honored other gods, and ignored the covenant. Israel's idolatrous rebellion demeaned Yahweh and brought shame upon the nation.

[God] laid low the flower of Israel . . .
So he made their days vanish like a breath [because] . . .
 Their heart was not steadfast toward him;
  they were not true to his covenant. . . .
They tested the Most High God,
  and rebelled against him.
They did not observe his decrees,
   but turned away and were faithless like their ancestors;
   they twisted like a treacherous bow. (78:31, 33, 37, 56–57)

[Israel] served their idols,
  which became a snare to them. . . .
Thus they became unclean by their acts,
  and prostituted themselves in their doings. (106:36, 39)

Israel's shameful behavior was one source of disgrace. But righteous Israelites also experienced shame. Other nations plundered and taunted them. In those moments righteous psalmists lament their social shame.

How long, you people, shall my honor suffer shame? (4:2a)

I am a worm, and not human;
  scorned by others, and despised by the people. (22:6)

All day long my disgrace is before me,
  and shame has covered my face. (44:15)

You know the insults I receive,

and my shame and dishonor. (69:19)

It is for your sake that I have borne reproach,

that shame has covered my face.

I have become a stranger to my kindred (69:7–8a)

In sum, humans experience shame because of their lowliness before God, their disloyalty toward God, and humiliation from outsiders. However, God's people should not bear disgrace. When the righteous experience shame (either personally or corporately), this is a problem. Israel's shame violates the moral order established in the Sinai covenant—the faithful should be rewarded with blessings, favor, and honor.

Israel's dishonor jeopardizes God's own reputation as their patron. When Gentile nations attacked and humiliated Israel, they publicly challenged Yahweh's honor. So, the psalmists pray for God to vindicate Israel's honor for the sake of preserving his own reputation.

3. Honoring the Faithful

Many psalmists petition God to notice and remove their shame. They expect God to vindicate their honor.

O my God, in you I trust;

   do not let me be put to shame;

   do not let my enemies exult over me.

Do not let those who wait for you be put to shame. (25:2–3a)

O guard my life, and deliver me;

   do not let me be put to shame. (25:20)

Do not make me the scorn of the fool. (39:8)

In you, O LORD, I seek refuge;

   do not let me ever be put to shame;

   in your righteousness deliver me. (31:1)

Do not let me be put to shame, O LORD,

   for I call on you. (31:17a)

Do not let those who hope in you be shamed because of me,

   O Lord GOD of hosts;

do not let those who seek you be dishonored because of me,

   O God of Israel. (69:6)

In you, O LORD, I take refuge;

   let me never be put to shame. . . .

You will increase my honor,

   and comfort me once again. (71:1, 21)

Do not let the downtrodden be put to shame;

   let the poor and needy praise your name. (74:21)

Several psalms claim that God honors people because of their obedience. These passages reinforce the idea that God keeps covenant with those who also keep covenant with him. People aligned with God's honor can expect his saving intervention. The expectation of future honor is a motivation for virtue and covenant obedience.

> Vindicate me, O LORD,
>> for I have walked in my integrity,
>> and I have trusted in the Lord without wavering. (26:1)

> Look to him, and be radiant;
>> so your faces shall never be ashamed. (34:5)

> The LORD knows the days of the blameless,
>> and their heritage will abide forever;
> they are not put to shame in evil times,
>> in the days of famine they have abundance. (37:18–19)

> Then I shall not be put to shame,
>> having my eyes fixed on all your commandments. (119:6)

> May my heart be blameless in your statutes,
>> so that I may not be put to shame. (119:80)

In the psalms, vindication occurs mostly during the present age. God eliminates political opponents, restores land, preserves children, and grants prosperity. However, Psalms 49 and 73 anticipate an eschatological honor for God's people.

4. Honoring the King

The messianic psalms (2, 45, 72, 89, 110) envision the exaltation of David's royal family above all other kings. God has honored the Davidic king as his favored son and appointed him to rule as his royal representative over the earth (2:7–10).

> For you [God] meet [the king] with rich blessings;
>   you set a crown of fine gold on his head. . . .
> His glory is great through your help;
>   splendor and majesty you bestow on him. (21:3, 5)

> [To the king:]
> God has blessed you forever.
> Gird your sword on your thigh, O mighty one,
>   in your glory and majesty. . . .
> God, your God, has anointed you
>   with the oil of gladness beyond your companions; . . .
> I will cause your name to be celebrated in all generations;
>   therefore the peoples will praise you forever and ever.
> (45:2–3, 7, 17)

> May his name endure forever,
>   his fame continue as long as the sun. (72:17)

I will make him the firstborn,
the highest of the kings of the earth. (89:27)

The Lord says to my lord,
"Sit at my right hand
until I make your enemies your footstool." (110:1)

[David's] enemies I will clothe with disgrace,
but on him, his crown will gleam. (132:18)

Israel's king was honored to mediate Gods' kingdom rule on earth. The king administered God's salvation to the world. This meant implementing God's honor code by assigning people to their proper status. The king demoted enemies and helped the dispossessed.

May he defend the cause of the poor of the people,
give deliverance to the needy,
and crush the oppressor. (72:4)

David's family lost the honorable standing that God had bestowed. The kings of Israel were unfaithful to the covenant, so God rejected and shamed them.

You have removed the scepter from his hand,
and hurled his throne to the ground.
You have cut short the days of his youth;
you have covered him with shame. (89:44–45)

5. *Shaming the Enemies*

Imprecatory psalms ask God to shame enemies. The recompense for opposing God and his people is disgrace and humiliation. Many psalms request that God's shaming judgment occur soon.

> Let them be put to shame and dishonor
>> who seek after my life. (35:4)

> Let those who exalt themselves against me
>> be clothed with shame and dishonor. (35:6)

> Let all those be put to shame and confusion
>> who seek to snatch away my life;
> let those be turned back and brought to dishonor
>> who desire my hurt. (40:14, cf. 70:2)

> Let my accusers be put to shame and consumed;
>> let those who seek to hurt me
>> be covered with scorn and disgrace. (71:13)

> Fill their faces with shame,
>> so that they may seek your name, O Lord.
> Let them be put to shame and dismayed forever;
>> let them perish in disgrace. (83:16–17)

May my accusers be clothed with dishonor;
> may they be wrapped in their own shame as in a mantle.
(109:29)

May all who hate Zion
> be put to shame and turned backward. (129:5)

Several psalms express confidence that God will indeed put opponents to shame.

All my enemies shall be ashamed and struck with terror;
> they shall turn back, and in a moment be put to shame.
(6:10)

For God will scatter the bones of the ungodly;
> they will be put to shame, for God has rejected them. (53:5)

All worshipers of images are put to shame. (97:7)

The blatant cursing of others may seem uncouth for modern readers. However, the public shaming of enemies was an inevitable aspect of God's covenant relationship with Israel. God diminished other nations in order to exalt his favored nation. To rescue Israel from bondage, God must defeat the enemy. Such imprecations were not merciless requests for revenge but rather petitions for God to rebalance this unjust world and restore the social order. They wanted God to act honorably.

These five socio-theological motifs appear in many psalms. Yet, the book of Psalms remains a collection of individual songs. Each psalm was composed for a specific occasion. For this reason, the next section includes a brief introduction to the specific social and ideological situation for each of the fifteen psalms.

Further Resources

To learn more about honor and shame in the Psalms, refer to these academic articles:

- deSilva, David. "Honor and Shame." Pages 287–300 in *Dictionary of the Old Testament: Wisdom, Poetry & Writings*, ed. Tremper Longman and Peter Enns. Downers Grove, IL: IVP Academic, 2008.
- Shramek, Dustin. "Honor and Shame in the Psalter." Unpublished paper. Accessed January 20, 2014. http://hispeaceuponus.files.wordpress.com/2009/08/honor-and-shame-in-the-psalter1.pdf.

These articles analyze honor-shame in specific psalms:

- Botha, Phil J. "A Social-Scientific Reading of Psalm 129." *HTS* 58 (2002): 1401–14.
- _____. "Psalm 67 in Its Literary and Ideological Context." *OTE* 17 (2004): 365–79.
- _____. "Psalm 118 and Social Values in Ancient Israel." *OTE* 16 (2003): 195–215.

- _____. "'The Honour of the Righteous Will Be Restored': Psalm 75 in Its Social Context." *OTE* 15 (2002): 320–334.

- _____. "Shame and the Social Setting of Psalm 119." *OTE* 12 (1999): 389–400.

- _____. "The 'Enthronement Psalms': A Claim to the World-Wide Honour of Yahweh." *OTE*, 1998, 24–39.

- _____. "To Honour Yahweh in the Face of Adversity: A Socio-Critical Analysis of Psalm 131." *Skrifen Kerk* 19 (1998): 525–33.

- Mare, Leonard. "Honour and Shame in Psalm 44." *Scriptura* 113 (2014): 1–12.

- Tucker, W Dennis, Jr. "Is Shame a Matter of Patronage in the Communal Laments?" *JSOT* 31 (2007): 465–80.

Psalm 8: The Glorious Honor Granted to Humans

This praise song of David marvels at God's lavish favor toward humans at creation. Psalm 8 functions as a biblical commentary on Genesis 1–2, as it explains the theological significance of the creation account. The very God who spoke the galaxies into place has crowned humans with honor and glory. Once dust, humans now enjoy dominion over creation. Our exalted position in the created order testifies to God's majesty as the world's supreme ruler.

O Lord, you are exalted as our supreme ruler;
your name is infinitely glorious in the entire world!
Your glory is higher than the heavens.
Even babies praise your greatness
and discredit the baseless taunts of enemies.[1-2]

I marvel at the majestic universe,
the amazing stars and infinite galaxies.
But amidst the entire universe,
you pay special attention to insignificant humans.
You breathed life into dust to make them your very image.
You have exalted them—they are virtually divine!
Your crowned their heads with glory and honor.

They enjoy an exalted position in your world.

You have shared your authority with humans over all creation; they rule over animals of the land, birds in the air, and fish of the sea.[3-8]

O Lord, you are the exalted ruler over everything.

Your name is infinitely glorious in the entire world![9]

Psalm 12: God's Promised Rescue for the Humiliated

This poem by David laments the subjugation of God's people. Though enemies taunt and demean, God vows to rescue his people from disgrace. This psalm highlights God's preference for the marginalized and humiliated. God identifies as a patron of the helpless and comforter of the shamed.

O Lord, I need you to rescue me!
Nobody is devoted to your glory;
everyone loyal to your majesty has disappeared.[1]

People say outrageous lies;
they are two-faced smooth-talkers.
Please cut off their arrogant lips.
Their tongues boast in a false status,
They brag, "Our mouths are mighty and victorious;
we could rule over anyone!"[2-4]

But the Lord says,
"I will arise and take action.
The poor are humiliated and the needy mourn,
but nobody helps.
So I will rescue them from disgrace,

and bring them into my care."

The Lord's promises are always true;

they are solid like pure gold.

Though the wicked look to pounce on us

and people esteem their evil ways,

the Lord will rescue us;

he will protect us from these arrogant oppressors.[5-8]

Psalm 15: The Honor Code to Become God's Guests

This short hymn celebrates the ideal Yahweh worshiper. This type of person is considered honorable enough to enter into God's presence. Priests likely recounted this psalm at the entrance of the Jerusalem temple to prepare people for entering the holy space. The virtues in this psalm are not merely religious qualifications for temple entrance but were also esteemed as honorable characteristics within the community.

O Lord, who has the honor of being a guest in your house?

Who is worthy of standing in your presence?

Those who do these things will enjoy such a favored position:

- Live a noble life.
- Do what is virtuous before God.
- Say what is true.
- Esteem, don't slander, other people.
- Be loyal, not evil, to friends.
- Be respectful, not insulting, to neighbors.
- Shame those who are wicked.
- Honor those who revere the Lord.
- Stay true to promises always.
- Use wealth to help, not extort, the weak.
- Avoid corruption.

The person who does these things will be firmly established in a place of honor before you.

Psalm 23: The Divine Patron and Host

This popular hymn speaks about God's generous and honoring patronage. David uses two common metaphors to convey God's protection and provision for his people—God is both a shepherd and a host. These images worshipfully visualize Yahweh's patron-client relationship with Israel. God is faithful to always favor Israel with benevolence.

My patron is Yahweh.

He generously provides for my every need.

He gifts me the finest.

He brings me to the best places.

His perfect care delights my heart.

He gives wise guidance so that I'm never lost.

This lavish generosity makes his name great.[1-3]

Even when the clouds of shame and despair gather,

I do not worry,

because you, O God, have my back.

Your strong hand gives me complete assurance.[4]

You welcome me to a lavish banquet,

so everyone sees I'm your honored guest.

You exalt me to prominence;

your favor towards me reaches to the heavens.

Without any doubt, you faithfully provide for me every day.

You always extend hospitality and honor me with your presence.[5-6]

Psalm 25: Hope in God's Deliverance from Shame

This psalm of David combines elements of confession, lament, and petition to express hope in God's deliverance from shame. The psalm appears jumbled because the original Hebrew is structured alphabetically, not thematically. However, the psalm explores the causes and solutions of the psalmist's shame.

The author repeatedly acknowledges wrongdoing and asks God to release him from the shameful consequences of his covenant disobedience. His petition for help involves a two-pronged strategy. One, the author pledges future obedience; he promises to honor God by observing the covenant. Two, he magnifies the supremacy of God's own covenant loyalty. The psalmist hopes that God's faithfulness will override his own unfaithfulness. The promise of covenant obedience and the appeal to Gods' covenant loyalty express the author's hope that God will rescue him from shame.

O Lord, I rely upon you for help;
you are my only hope.
Save me from shame;
don't let my enemies disgrace me.
Don't shame those who hope in you;
shame those who do evil.

Make my heart follow your ways;

guide me with truth.

You are the God who rescues me;

I hope in your deliverance.

Remember your benevolence and covenant loyalties

which have always defined you.

Forget my disobedience and foolishness.

Display your covenant loyalty and rescue me

to prove your honorable character.[1-7]

The Lord is virtuous;

he instructs the wayward

and guides the teachable.

The people who keep covenant and honor you with obedience,

they will experience God's covenant loyalty and benevolent

provision.

To enhance the glory of your name, O Lord,

don't avenge my awful wrongdoings.

The Lord will guide those who esteem his name.

They will enjoy harmony and honor in the community;

their children will continue their name.

Covenant partnership is for those who esteem God's name;

he forms a special relationship with them.

I always hope in the Lord

to untangle my life from evil.[8-15]

Grant me favor,

for I am rejected and despised.

Give me peace and security.

Look upon my awful state

and forget my disobedience and disloyalty.

See how many people utterly despise me.

Protect and rescue me;

O my patron, deliver me from shame.

Stay true and remain trustworthy towards me,

because I hope in you for deliverance.

O God, restore the status of your people, Israel;

rescue them from all their misfortunes.[16-22]

Psalm 30: Praise for God's Rescue from Shame

This song of David praises God for rescue from destruction. The psalmist faced great shame at the hands of his enemies. But just when death seemed imminent, God intervened to deliver and exalt him. The psalm is written as a testimony of praise; it reflects upon a season of despair through the lens of God's benevolent provision. God removed shame and restored honor, so now the psalmist reciprocates by promising to declare God's praises forever.

O Lord, I will exalt you because you have exalted me.
You prevented my enemies from trampling on my face.
O Lord, I asked you to help,
and you restored me.
O Lord, you lifted me from the deepest pits
and redeemed my life from the grave.[1-3]

Sing his praises, you loyal subjects;
express your thankfulness to his awesome name.
God may appear absent and stingy for a bit,
but he always extends favor.
You might grieve for a night,
but then you'll celebrate again the next morning.

Because God has vindicated me,

I shall never be demoted.

Because of God's benevolence,

my standing is firmly established.[4–7a]

You hid your face from me,

and I was shamed.

Then I cried to you, O Lord:

"Will my death bring honor to your name?

Will my dead corpse sing your praises for your patronage?

Hear me, Lord, and extend your benevolence.

Be my patron!"

After I prayed this,

you turned my humiliation into celebration;

you removed my shame and restored my status

in order that my heart always praise you.

O Lord, I will always repay your benevolence with gratitude.[7b–12]

Psalm 44: Vindicating Israel's Shame and Appealing to God's Loyalty

This lament poem mourns the loss of national honor. After calamity erases Israel's privileged status as God's people, the nation calls upon God to honor his promises as their provider-patron. The psalm follows this structural logic:

- *God once favored and honored Israel (vv. 1–8),*
- *but now he has forsaken and shamed them (9–16)*
- *even though Israel has honored God (17–22),*
- *so God should vindicate Israel to save face (23–26).*

Psalm 44 applies the moral logic of patron-client relationships to Israel's covenant with Yahweh. God faithfully acted like a patron in protecting and exalting Israel, so Israel reciprocated with loyalty and honor. But Israel's current national disgrace implies that God is untrustworthy and unfaithful—the marks of a shameful patron. Israel's shame brings dishonor to God's name, for he appears weak and disloyal. In this situation, the patron must rescue his client to save face. When God vindicates Israel, he vindicates his own name.

Your name is famous, O God;
for generations our ancestors recounted your amazing works.
You cleansed our land of gentiles
then helped your favored people grow strong.

You dispossessed those other nations
but liberated your favored people.
Israel's own military did not conquer the land;
nor did their strength help them win.
But God's mighty hand secured the victory
because he favors his special people.
You, my God, are the sovereign ruler
who protects and exalts your people Israel.
With you we humiliate enemies;
with your name we vanquish opponents.
We do not hope in ourselves for exaltation,
because you alone rescued us from enemies,
and shamed our opponents.
In you, God, we have salvific honor forever.
And so we owe gratitude and praise to your glorious name.[1-8]

But despite all your past faithfulness to our covenant,
you, O God, have rejected and humiliated us.
You cause us to run away scared;
they have pillaged us.
With no protection, we are slaughtered like sheep.
With no backing, we are tossed around like pawns.
We appear worthless in your eyes;
you gave us away like useless trash.
You let our enemies mock and scoff at us;
they degrade and despise us.

Because of you, we are the butt of all their jokes;

all the nations treat us like crap.

We feel disgraced, all day, everyday.

Shame completely covers our face

because of all the humiliating things they say and do against

us.[9-16]

So why are we facing national shame, O God?

This is not our fault!

We have remained faithful to you;

we stayed true to our covenant relationship.

Our hearts have remained loyal to you;

we have obeyed your word from Moses.

But yet, you have made us to be nothing,

and placed us in darkness.

If we had betrayed your name,

or given your glory to a foreign god,

then of course we deserve this shame.

But we are butchered like sheep because of your disloyalty![17-22]

Wake up, God! Why are you sleeping now?

Rescue us from this shame!

Do not abandon and reject Israel forever.

Why have you turned your face away from us?

Why do you still withhold your favor from us?

Stop ignoring our humiliation.

Our faces are being shoved into the ground.

We have become worthless dirt.

Your covenant love is our help for restored honor.

Wake up and vindicate us from this shame;

prove that you are an honorable patron.[23-26]

Psalm 74: Restoring Israel to Vindicate God's Name from Shame

This psalm laments the destruction of the Jerusalem temple. Because of catastrophic disgrace, Israel accuses God of forgetting the covenant. Psalm 74 incorporates the same patron-client logic as Psalm 44—God the patron must save his client Israel, lest he lose face and be dishonored. Psalm 74 mentions how Gentile nations publicly shame God because of his failure to defend Israel. The enemies of God defile, revile, and mock his name. God must answer this honor challenge. Psalm 74 also appeals to God's creative power. In Genesis 1–2 God overcame chaos and disorder to put everything in the proper order, so now he should re-create the world by putting Israel (and their enemies) back where they belong in the social hierarchy. This psalm invites God to restore Israel in order to vindicate his own name.

O God, why do you reject us forever?
Why are you so vengeful against your own sheep?
Stay true to your flock Israel,
which you rescued from Egypt to make your special people.
Stay true to Jerusalem, your very home on earth.[1-2]

Look at the destruction of the Jerusalem temple.

The enemies have ravaged through your house;

they pillaged your holy place,

and taken over your sacred possession.

They demolished all the pillars with axes.

They smashed all the carvings with hammers.

They burned everything to the ground.

They have decimated your house and belittled your name.

They gloat, "We completely rule over those rejects!"

We have no home as a nation.

We have no sign of God's power or presence.

We are rejected and humiliated.[3-9]

How long, O Lord, will you let the enemy shame us?

Will they despise the glory of your name forever?

Why do you do nothing?

Why stay silent and let this happen?[10-11]

Nevertheless, our God is the ancient ruler of all;

he displays his sovereign, saving power in the whole world.

At creation you vanquished the forces of chaos,

and brought order to creation.

You destroyed the ancient monsters,

then fed their corpses to vultures.

You ordered all the waters into their place.

At creation you demoted darkness to create light;

you lifted the moon, sun, and stars into their position.
You have put everything in the right place.[12-17]

If you are powerful enough to order the universe,
then re-create the world.
Like you did at creation,
vanquish your enemies and restore order.
Look at how the enemy demeans and disgraces;
those shameless people trample upon your name.
Don't abandon your sheep to the wolves for destruction;
don't forsake your people.
Remember our special relationship and your covenant
promises,
because darkness and cruelty fill our land.
Your people are dispossessed;
don't let us be openly disgraced.
Rescue us so that we can exalt your glorious name.
Take action, O God; defend your honor.
Notice how those shameless enemies spit upon your face.
Respond to the taunts of your opponents
who keep insulting your name.[18-23]

Psalm 75: God as the Sole Decider of Honor Status

This hymn praises God's sovereign power to determine the honor and status of all people. The wicked have arrogantly presumed an exalted status ("boast," "lift their horn"), but God will subdue them ("pour his cup," "cut their horns") and vindicate his people. His judgments will rectify the social order by putting everyone into the right place. This psalm praises God for his exclusive authority to honor his people.

We owe you gratitude, O God.

We give you thanks.

We always mention your glorious name to others,

because of your enduring loyalty and benevolence towards us.[1]

God declares:

On the day that I decide,

I will make everything right,

and put everyone in their place.

If the whole world descends into chaos,

I myself will maintain order.

I say to the arrogant and evil:

- Do not make ridiculous honor claims about yourself.
- Do not exalt yourself.

- Do not assume positions of glory.
- Do not speak with disdain over others.[2-3]

No person in the entire world can exalt themselves to honor.

But only God determines a person's status;

he shames one and honors another.

God alone has the prerogative to promote and demote.

God holds the cup of humiliation in his hand;

he is ready to pour it out.

Evildoers will drink that cup down to the last sip,

and be filled with disgrace.[4-8]

But compared to them,

I will celebrate you forever;

I will honor the God of Israel with praise.

For God will debase those who exalt themselves,

and honor his covenant people.[9-10]

Psalm 89: The Restoration of David's King from Shame to Honor

This communal lament mourns the tragic downfall of Israel's king. The head of Israel, God's own representative, bore international disgrace—this was a political and theological crisis for Israel. The psalm follows this structural logic:

- *The mighty God who favored Israel (vv. 1–18)*
- *covenanted an enduring and exalted dynasty to David (19–37),*
- *but he forgot those promises (38–45),*
- *so Israel pleas for God to restore David's crown (46–51).*

In 2 Samuel 7 Yahweh covenanted to establish and protect David's family as Israel's kings. But the king's disgrace during the Babylonian captivity contradicted God's promise to exalt David. God was being an unfaithful patron to his client-king David.

The humiliation of the king impacted the entire nation. Collectivistic cultures have a sense of corporate solidarity—the head represents the entire group. The king's fallen crown brought shame to all of Israel. And since the king brokered God's covenant blessings, his captivity meant Israel would no longer receive Yahweh's favor. These dynamics explain the political and theological crisis of an exiled Davidic king and why the psalmist petitions God to restore David's crown.

I will forever sing about your constant patronage to us;

my lips will declare your covenant faithfulness to everyone.

Your loyalty toward Israel is eternal;

your faithfulness is rock solid.

You promised, "I have a covenant relationship

with my specially chosen ruler, King David.

All your children will rule as kings;

your royal dynasty will last forever."[1-2]

Let the whole world praise your amazing works, Lord;

let the people sing of your covenant faithfulness.

Nothing in the world is like the Lord;

no one in the heavens is like the Lord.

You are respected by the angelic council;

you are exalted over everyone around you.

O Lord of the angelic armies in heaven,

no one has authority to rule like you.

You are defined by your covenant faithfulness to us.

You are supreme over tribal gods and sea monsters,

obliterating them to nothing.

Your hand brings order to our chaotic world.

All of creation submits to your rule;

your authority covers every square inch of reality,

from the north to the south.

Even mountain peaks praise your glorious name.[3-12]

Your strong arm always delivers;

your hand reigns supreme over all.

Vindication and loyalty define your kingly rule.

Israelites who celebrate in the temple are full of joy;

they live in the light of your intimate presence.

They make your name great all day long,

and magnify your name for all the covenant favors.

You are establishing your domain over the whole world,

first at creation, and now through David's family.

Our victory is your glory.

Our exaltation over enemies is a gift from you.

Our protection comes from you alone.

Our kings establish your benevolent rule.[13-18]

You, O God, promised to your servant David,

"I have crowned a mighty person;

I have exalted my chosen man.

I have raised up my client-king David,

and appointed him to rule with glory and honor.

My hand will always strengthen him.

No enemy will deceive or humiliate him.

I will subjugate and obliterate his opponents.

I promise to always be a faithful and trustworthy patron.

Because of my name,

David's throne will be honored.

I will grant him authority over the entire world.

Then David will sing praises to honor me:

'God, you are my patron-father;

you always exalt me.'

I will make David my special king,

the highest ruler, king over all other kings.

My covenant loyalty will stand forever;

our special relationship will always endure.

I promise that his dynasty will rule forever,

and his throne will always be prominent.

If his children disobey my word and ignore my instructions,

if they turn away from me and are disloyal,

then there will be consequences—

David's successors will be demoted.

But even then, I promise that my covenant loyalty will continue.

I will honor my original word to David;

I will keep our covenant.

I will stay true to my promises.

By my awesome splendor,

I have forever sworn to exalt David's family.

I will stay true and keep faith.

His children will rule forever;

their throne will be established until the end of time."[19-37]

God, you guaranteed great honor to David,

but you have broken all your promises.

You have abandoned and rejected David's throne;

you now despise your appointed ruler.

You have forsaken the covenant with your client-king;

you have thrown David's crown down into the dirt.

You have invaded his capital;

you have destroyed his empire.

His royal courts are raped and pillaged.

The surrounding nations mock and insult our king.

You exalted our enemies—not us!—to positions of honor.

They celebrate with victory feasts.

And your hand has been absent.

You have not protected or delivered the king.

You grabbed the scepter out of his hand

and threw it to the ground.

You have ended his glorious rule.

Because of you, the king is covered with shame.[38-45]

How long, O Lord, will you remain absent?

Will you despise your own people forever?

Remember that my days are numbered;

I will die soon—so act quickly!

Lord, show us your covenant loyalty.

You promised to David to always be faithful.

Look, Lord, your king is disgraced.

My heart resents the shame we now face.

The enemies degrade us;

they humiliate us and your king.

May you, O Lord, always be praised. Amen. [46-51]

Psalm 96: A Declaration of God's Universal Honor

The enthronement psalms (47, 93, and 96–99) declare the universal honor of Israel's God. Yahweh is the king sitting upon his majestic throne and ruling over the entire world. This God who created the world requires worship and exaltation from all peoples. The kingship of God—a metaphor for honor—means God is exalted to the highest position, so his subjects must respect and honor him.

Psalm 96 calls all nations to glorify God because of his supremacy over other gods. Yahweh, the world's true king, deserves honor because of his royal power to create, rule, and judge. Every aspect of creation must pay homage to his glorious name. In declaring God's sovereign honor, the psalmist trusts that God will eventually restore the honor of his people.

Sing new praises to the Lord;
everyone, sing praises to the Lord.
Sing the Lord's praises;
magnify the honor of his name;
proclaim the glories of his patronage every day.
Declare his awesome glory to the entire world,
and his benevolent deeds to all peoples.
The Lord is so great

and deserves great praise.

He must be highly exalted,

honored above all other gods.

Their gods are just lifeless, impotent figurines;

yet our God created the world.

Honor and glory define his fullness;

authority and splendor fill his presence.[1-6]

O peoples of the world, honor the Lord;

honor his glory and authority.

Honor his glorious name;

bring your gifts into his presence.

Esteem his infinite worth;

he is the Lord of perfect splendor!

Declare this to all peoples:

"Our God rules the world,

and so I swear my allegiance to him alone!"

He put the world in its place;

nothing can overrule his sovereign authority.

He will appoint all peoples to their right status.

May the entire world celebrate this great news;

let all creation—land, sea, and sky—exult in the Lord,

for he comes to set everything right;

he will put everyone in their true place.

His glorious judgments will vindicate his people

and display his sovereign authority over all.[7-12]

Psalm 109: A Plea for Personal Vindication and Vengeance against Shamers

This imprecatory poem of David asks God for vengeance and vindication. The false accusations of an enemy have publicly slandered the psalmist (vv. 1–5), so he asks God to smear the enemy with shame (6–15). These curses erase the core symbols of a person's status—children, land, and name. The enemy deserves such disgrace because he has dishonored others (16–20). This main portion of the psalm prays for vengeance—the humiliation of an opponent; the final section (21–29) prays for vindication— the exaltation of the psalmist.

O God, whom I exalt with praise,
wake up and vindicate me!
Evil, lying tongues are defaming my name;
they scorn me with hateful words.
They repay my kindness with slander,
even while I pray for them.
Those ingrates repay my love with hate;
those traitors publicly disgrace me.[1-5]

So curse my enemy with shame.

- May his name be defamed.
- May the judge denounce him.

63

- May he die soon.

- May another person replace him.

- May his children be orphans.

- May his wife be a widow.

- May his descendants be beggars.

- May his family become homeless.

- May the bank seize his assets.

- May foreigners plunder his land.

- May everyone reject him.

- May everybody scorn his children.

- May his descendants die off.

- May his name cease to exist.

- May God punish him for his parents' sin.

- May he be completely forgotten.

- May he become nothing, a complete disgrace.[6-15]

He deserves such shame for good reasons:

- He was stingy and took advantage of the needy.

- He loved to disgrace, so let disgrace come upon him.

- He never honored, so let honor depart from him.

- He covered others with shame, so let shame clothe him.

May disgrace be the recompense
for those who dishonor me.[16-20]

O Lord, my patron,
to preserve the honor of your name, help me!

to show your covenant loyalty, rescue me!

I am oppressed and depressed.

I am nothing but a shadow.

I am flicked away like a bug.

My entire being is becoming nothing.

My enemies disgrace me;

they mock me whenever they walk by.

Help me, O Lord, my patron.

Rescue me to show your covenant loyalty;

display your benevolence so everyone respects you.

They might shame me,

but you shall honor me.

May they be disgraced,

and may I gain face.[21-29]

I will express my gratitude to the Lord;

I will sing his praises to everyone,

because he faithfully stands with the desperate

and rescues them from great shame.[30-31]

Psalm 113: Praising the Honorable and Honoring God

This hymn praises God for his majestic glory and kindness toward the lowly. The psalm consists of three equal parts: God deserves glory always and everywhere (vv. 1–3), for he is exalted above everything (4–6), yet this majestic king bestows honor upon the lowly (vv. 7–9). In other words, "For though the Lord is high, he regards the lowly" (138:6a). Psalm 113 offers a succinct summary of the psalm's honor-shame theology—honor God because he is honorable and honoring.

Declare praises to the Lord.

Declare his praises, you who depend on the Lord.

Give honor to the glorious name of the Lord,

from now until the end of time.

From the sunrise to the sunset,

sing praises to the glorious name of the Lord.[1-3]

For the Lord is exalted high above all the other peoples.

His magnificent glory extends above the heavens.

No one is like the Lord our God;

he reigns from his throne with supreme honor.

He is so high that the heavens are beneath him.[4-6]

Yet this majestic king raises the disgraced out of the dirt.

He rescues the shamed from humiliation.

He exalts them to positions of royalty;

they sit enthroned as his princes.

For example, he honors barren a woman with family

so she can celebrate motherhood.

Declare praises to the Lord.[7-]

Psalm 129: The Reversal of Shameful Affliction

This communal thanksgiving celebrates God's rescue after a long period of disgrace and hostility (probably the Babylonian exile). Israel experienced national shame as exiles in bondage, but God has now restored their proper honor. An aspect of Israel's exaltation is praying for the humiliation of enemies. This song cultivates a sense of group solidarity among Israelites, who once endured shame but are now resolved to assert their honor.

Our enemies kept attacking us, says Israel.
Our enemies kept attacking,
but they did not overcome us.
They plowed right over us;
they smashed our face into the dirt.
Yet the Lord is faithful to rescue from humiliation;
he has redeemed us from bondage.[1-4]

May all those who despise Israel face great shame
and run away humiliated.
May our enemies be scorched like dry grass
and wither to nothing.

May onlookers never say to them,

"Wow, God has really honored you!

May the Lord favor his people!"[5-8]

Psalm 146: God as the True Patron

This psalm is a general exhortation to trust in God as the world's true patron. He powerfully and faithfully provides for his people, especially those who face oppression and rejection. Therefore, people must be loyal clients who exalt and honor God for his generous provision.

Sing the Lord's praises to honor him.
My heart sings the Lord's praises to exalt him.
I will forever sing the Lord's praises to esteem him.[1-2]

Never put your hope in humans rulers for rescue;
they never deliver on their promises;
they are weak and mortal.[3-4]

Instead, exult in your God, the true patron;
put all of your hope in the Lord.
Because he alone has the power to make the entire world—
land, sky, sea, and everything in them;
plus, he is faithful to keep his covenant promises forever.
The Lord vindicates the oppressed from the margins.
He provides for the hungry and afflicted.
He liberates those trapped in bondage.
He restores the maimed.

He honors the shamed

and exalts the lowly.

He generously favors his people.

He protects vulnerable immigrants.

He takes care of the needy

but turns the oppressive into nothing.

This is how Israel's God shows his supremacy and glory forever.

Sing the Lord's praise to honor him.[5-10]

Thanks for reading this book. I hope you enjoyed reading it as much as I enjoyed writing it. If you think the book may be helpful to others, please consider writing an honest view at Amazon.com. Thanks! ~Jayson

To learn more about the Honor-Shame Paraphrase series, you can visit:

 HonorShame.com/HSP

CPSIA information can be obtained
at www.ICGtesting.com
Printed in the USA
LVHW012326051118
596096LV00007B/285/P